MY   '10

ACTION SPORTS

ROCK CLIMBING

Tom Greve

ROURKE PUBLISHING
Vero Beach, Florida 32964

www.rourkepublishing.com

PHOTO CREDITS: © Nick Schlax: Title Page; © MistikaS: 3; © YoavPeled: 4; © Paul Zizka: 5; © Goran Kuzmanovski: 6, 10, 19; © brannend: 7; © Krisztian Szalay: 8; © Frances A. Miller: 8; © Michael Zysman: 11; © Jason Maehl: 11; © Claudio Baldini: 11; © worldinmyeyes.pl: 11; © Sean O. S. Barley: 12; © Paulo Resende: 13; © Galyna Andrushko: 14; © Associated Press: 15, 17; © lxd: 16; © Waniuszka: 18; © GeoM: 20; © urosr: 20; © Iurii: 21; © Rich Legg: 22

Edited by Jeanne Sturm

Cover and Interior designed by Tara Raymo

Library of Congress Cataloging-in-Publication Data

Greve, Tom.
  Rock climbing / Tom Greve.
     p. cm. -- (Action sports)
  Includes index.
  ISBN 978-1-60694-363-2
  1. Rock climbing--Juvenile literature. I. Title.
  GV200.2.G78 2009
  796.522'3--dc22
                                    2009006061

Printed in the USA

CG/CG

www.rourkepublishing.com - rourke@rourkepublishing.com
Post Office Box 643328 Vero Beach, Florida 32964

TABLE OF CONTENTS

The View is Always Best from the Top

Some people like to test the boundaries of their **physical** world. They like to know how far they can go, or how fast, or how high. Rock climbing is a sport that requires people to push the limits of their own strength and concentration to get to the top of something. Rock climbers enjoy the outdoors and are not afraid of heights. Climbers who master various techniques sometimes turn to **mountaineering** for the thrill of standing atop a mountain peak.

Why Climb?

Why do people climb rocks or mountains? For many, it's the thrilling challenge of using their own skills to conquer something so massive.

There are numerous categories of rock climbing. Bouldering is rock climbing without ropes or equipment. **Top-roping** involves two climbers using **harnesses**, ropes, **belaying** devices, and other climbing tools to get to the top of a steep rock formation or wall.

Mountaineering combines rock-climbing techniques and other skills to reach the top of a mountain. All climbing is dangerous, **exhausting**, and thrilling at the same time.

Bouldering requires great strength in a climber's fingers and toes.

Did You Know?

Strength alone will not make someone a good climber. Intense concentration, balance, and patience all come into play on successful climbs.

There are other forms of climbing as well. But no matter the style, climbing is always about getting from the bottom of something to the top.

Indoor Climbing

Many young rock climbers start by learning skills at indoor climbing courses. These climbing walls often have ropes attached and include bouldering courses. They provide opportunities to learn skills with fewer dangers than outdoor climbing.

Unlike outdoor climbs, changes in the weather do not affect indoor climbers.

Climbing walls vary in height and difficulty.

Outdoor Climbing

Bouldering is simply climbing up a **vertical** surface with almost no climbing equipment. It requires strong hands, good balance, and concentration. Bouldering can be dangerous, so climbers should use a **spotter**.

Climbers put chalk on their hands to keep them from getting slippery when they sweat.

Safety Helmet

A Climber's Equipment

Climbing Rope

Carabineer

Chalk Bag

11

Many climbers use a technical climbing **strategy** called top-roping. It is a relatively safe way to climb because the climbers use harnesses, ropes, and belaying devices to keep each other from falling all the way to the ground. It involves two climbers. One is the climber; the other is the belayer.

Climber

Belayer

Before a top-rope climb, one of the climbers hikes to the top to place an anchor into the rock. The rope is connected to the anchor during the climb.

Figure 8

Belaying devices create friction when the rope is threaded through them. The friction slows the rope down.

Belaying devices help control the movement of the climber's rope. They can pinch, and serve as a gentle brake on the rope in the event of a fall, so the climber only falls the length of the rope—not all the way to the ground.

Advanced climbers sometimes turn to mountaineering for the thrill of standing atop a mountain summit. Mountaineers do much more than just climb. They have to understand and adjust to the effects of **altitude** on their bodies. They need to react to changing weather conditions and recognize when a climb becomes too dangerous to continue.

Did You Know?

The highest mountains in the world are the Himalayas in Asia.

Top Climbers

Sir Edmund Hillary was a rock climber and mountaineer from New Zealand. In May of 1953, he and climbing companion Tenzing Norgay became the first people to climb to the top of Everest. It is among the great accomplishments in the history of climbing and land exploration on Earth.

Did You Know?

After conquering Everest, Sir Edmund Hillary worked to build schools and hospitals for the people living near Mount Everest. He died in January 2008.

Some of the world's **elite** mountain climbers try to reach the top of the highest mountain peak—or summit—on each of the world's seven **continents**. They refer to these peaks as the *Seven Summits*.

Continent	Summit	Height
Asia	Everest	29,029 feet (8,848 meters)
South America	Aconcagua	22,841 feet (6,962 meters)
North America	McKinley	20,320 feet (6,194 meters)
Africa	Kilimanjaro	19,341 feet (5,895 meters)
Europe	Elbrus	18,510 feet (5,642 meters)
Antarctica	Vinson Massif	16,050 feet (4,892 meters)
Australia	Kosciuszko	7,310 feet (2,228 meters)

Mountaineering involves **harsh** conditions in **remote** places. At higher elevations, there is less **oxygen** in the air. This affects a climber's body and mind. The lack of oxygen can make climbers sick. Sudden weather changes are also a constant threat high on a mountain.

Climbing mountains several miles high requires lots of time, planning, and equipment.

The view from the top of a climb can make all the work and the dangers seem worthwhile.

Climbing takes people to some of the most scenic places in the world. Aside from the world's tallest mountain summits, many rock outcroppings and formations provide a soul-stirring setting for climbs.

Did You Know?

No rock? No problem. In recent years, ice climbing has become popular. It involves many of the same skills as rock climbing, only on frozen waterfalls or vertical ice patches rather than solid rock.

So You Want to Be a Rock Climber?

Few action sports require the single-minded determination of rock climbing. The threat of falling pushes the climber to focus on every detail of his or her actions. The thrill of reaching the top of a rock formation, boulder, or even mountain peak is the ultimate climber's reward.

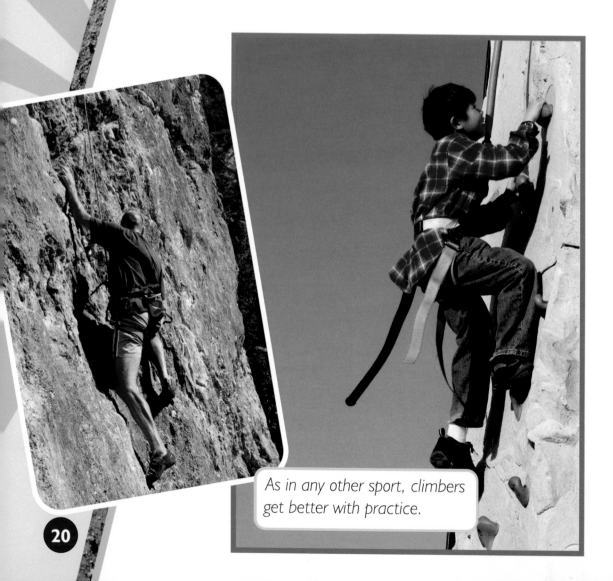

As in any other sport, climbers get better with practice.

Mountain climbers must balance their intese desire to reach a mountaintop against their best judgement regarding time and potentially dangerous conditions.

When climbing in a group, communication between climbers is important. Climbers have to be able and willing to trust each other in order to reach their destination.

Do you enjoy the outdoors and get a thrill out of finding your way up a tree or structure? If you do, then find a local climbing wall and give it a go. You may decide rock climbing is an action sport for you.

Glossary

altitude (AL-ti-tood): the height of something above ground level

belaying (buh-LAY-ing): a rock climbing rope-control technique that prevents a climber from falling to the ground

continents (KON-tuh-nuhnts): the seven large land masses of the Earth comprised of Europe, Asia, Africa, North America, South America, Australia, and Antarctica

elite (i-LEET): a group of exceedingly skilled individuals

exhausting (eg-ZAWST-ing): anything that leaves a person very tired

harnesses (HAR-niss-uz): arrangements of straps around climbers' waists and legs which connect to ropes

harsh (HARSH): unpleasant and hard on the body or senses

mountaineering (moun-tuh-NIHR-ing): climbing mountains for sport

oxygen (OK-suh-juhn): a colorless gas found in the air which humans and animals need in order to live

physical (FIZ-uh-kuhl): having to do with nature or natural objects

remote (ri-MOHT): far away, distant, removed from other things

spotter (SPOT-uhr): a person who stands below a climber ready to catch him or break his fall

strategy (STRAT-uh-jee): a plan used to achieve a goal

top-roping (TOP-rohp-ing): a two-person rock climbing technique using harnesses, ropes, and belay devices

vertical (VUR-tuh-kuhl): upright, or straight up and down

23

Index

Websites

www.kidzworld.com/article/3668-rock-climbing-gear
www.rock-climbing-for-life.com/rock_climbing_101.html
www.pbs.org/wgbh/nova/everest/history/southside.html
www.timeforkids.com/TFK/kids/news/story/0,28277,1702826,00.html

About the Author

Tom Greve lives in Chicago with his wife, Meg, and their children Madison and William. He enjoys bouldering in the Sandia Mountain foothills outside Albuquerque, New Mexico.